Financial Inclusion among Marginalized Women

A Case Study of Female Sex Workers at Ahmedabad

AUTHORED BY

Litty

Assistant Professor

Department of Studies in Social Management

Central University of Gujarat, India

ALLIED PUBLISHERS PVT. LTD.

Noida • Mumbai • Kolkata • Chennai • Bangalore

ALLIED PUBLISHERS PRIVATE LIMITED

D-5, Sector-2, **Noida**–201 301
Ph. Nos.: 0120-4320295/2542557/4352866
E-mail: delhi.books@alliedpublishers.com

17 Chittaranjan Avenue, **Kolkata**–700072
Ph.: 033-22129618 • E-mail: cal.books@alliedpublishers.com

15 J.N. Heredia Marg, Ballard Estate, **Mumbai**–400001
Ph.: 022-42126969 • E-mail: mumbai.books@alliedpublishers.com

No. 25/10, Commander-in-Chief Road, Ethiraj Lane (Next to Post Office)
Egmore, **Chennai**–600008
Ph.: 044-28223938 • E-mail: chennai.books@alliedpublishers.com

P.B. No. 9932, No. 15, 3rd Floor (Next to Vijaya Bank), 5th Cross, Gandhinagar,
Karnataka, **Bangalore**–560009. Ph.: 080-41530285/22386239
E-mail: bngl.books@alliedpublishers.com

Website: www.alliedpublishers.com

ISBN: 978-93-89934-66-3

Published by Sunil Sachdev and printed by Ravi Sachdev
at Allied Publishers Pvt. Ltd., D-5, Sector-2, Noida–201 301

Financial Inclusion among Marginalized Women

A Case Study of Female Sex Workers at Ahmedabad

Preface

Inequalities of various kinds shroud our daily lives. However, it creates greater vulnerabilities for many who were already marginalised. This is what Capabilities Approach also suggests that it is possible to attain greater Functionings if there is a choice available and exercised towards enhancing the right capabilities (Sen, 1984 and Nussbaum, 2000).

The first chapter focuses on deliberations about financial inclusion particularly in India. The second chapter in the current discussion is titled the veil of ignorance from two perspectives which are very contradicting from each other and yet applicable in the present study. The first approach is that the ignorance of people with respect to sex work makes it difficult for the sector to get formalised and acceptable in the society. So, it requires mass awareness through discussions in academic circles and other public discourses that will enable sex workers to function in this profession smoothly. The second aspect of 'veil of ignorance' is very much ingrained in sociological theory as advocated by John Rawls. He suggests that since situations and circumstances are different for every individual and groups, there is a difference in how people perceive and agree upon social contracts and how governing of work takes place. Therefore, one needs to sit behind the veil of ignorance so that we distance ourselves from our identity and then objectively analyse the situation for advocating policies for others particularly the disadvantaged groups to work with liberty (Rawls, 2001).

Subsequent chapters discuss the detailed history, findings, conclusion and recommendations of the study. Various countries have different positions towards prostitution with respect to its legality. Around 69 countries prostitution is illegal, in 39 countries prostitution is restricted or having limited legality, it is legal in 54 countries and in 1 country there is no law for prostitution (World Population Review, 2025). In India, prostitution is not a criminal offense but soliciting prostitution and prostitution in a public place is illegal. If prostitution is legal then sex workers could be covered under social security schemes. There are more than 8.25 lakh identified sex workers in India. Not many of them want to be in this trade by choice. Now, this situation puts them into a very vulnerable situation particularly with respect to their finances. Many of these FSWs would not be able to access formal financial institutions and therefore, may be prone to the exploitative powers of informal money lenders. The current book studies how financial inclusion initiatives have operated for FSWs in Ahmedabad city. Also, it looks into the history of the city of Ahmedabad and how it has brought many into the profession. The role of various stakeholders is also explored throughout the discussions in the book.

Acknowledgement

What is right and what is wrong is often just a perception based on what we have seen from far, heard from others and assumed based on what we have consumed from media. As we take up the discussion of female sex workers (FSWs) in this book, I would be content if this prepares the minds of readers to free up biases and think openly about favourable policies and practices for the FSWs.

This book is the outcome of a research project undertaken through the funding granted by Gargi – Centre for Holistic Development of Women, Dr. Babasaheb Ambedkar Open University, Ahmedabad. A research project is a product of collaborative efforts of many hands and institutions. I have a list of institutions and people to acknowledge for the final outcome of the project work.

First and foremost, I would like to thank the Vice Chancellor and her whole team at Dr. Babasaheb Ambedkar Open University and particularly Gargi - Centre for the Holistic Development of Women who funded the project. The topic being so significant yet not deliberated much, makes it all the more commendable an approach from the Centre and the University to encourage such research works.

Words wouldn't suffice to thank Prof. Gaurang Jani, retired Professor in Sociology, Gujarat University, who extended his whole hearted support to me each time I contacted him whether on phone or personally for understanding some facets of work and dealing with the utter non-availability of data in the sector. He generously lent me all his previous studies in this area to refer and quote. It was his expertise and experience of research in sex work industry that helped me to put this project in the current form.

Prof. Jani also contributed immensely for the panel discussion held as a part of the study to discuss the well being policies that could be for Female Sex Workers (FSWs). I also extend my heartfelt thanks to Prof. Rajesh Mackwana, Professor, Central

University of Gujarat, Dr. Awa Shukla, Director I/c- Student Services, Dr. Babasaheb Ambedkar Open University and Dr. Ishmeet Kaur, Assistant Professor, Central University of Gujarat to have contributed to the panel discussions by providing their learned insights for the study.

As mentioned in the report, availability of data and tracing the respondents would have been next to impossible without the CBO's help. I am indebted to SakhiJyot, CBO and all associated with the CBO who directly or indirectly helped me to collect and analyse my data in the right perspective. I would like to mention the names of Ms. Dipikaben, Ms. Manekben and Ms. Parasben particularly for helping me in every way that could be particularly for data collection.

I am also obliged to various officials from government departments and other NGOs which I contacted for having shared their perspectives and information in the research areas.

At the end I am grateful to my University for all the support provided. I earnestly thank Honourable Vice Chancellor, Prof. Rama Shankar Dubey and Registrar, Prof. H.B. Patel, Central University of Gujarat for the permissions and the infrastructure support to complete the project.

Also acknowledging the publication house, Allied Publishers who meticulously followed me up for completing the work and presenting with a reader-friendly approach.

Indebted to my family and friends too who always encourage me to do good work.

Litty Denis

Contents

CHAPTER 1

Financial Inclusion in India: A Progressive Story

Introduction

Universal financial inclusion is a long journey travelled bit by bit through successes and failures in multitude of project initiatives co-piloted by many leaders of government and non-government organisations who visualised financial inclusion as the foundation for human development. In developed countries it might still not be a point of major contention but for developing countries financial inclusion has to be a very well planned and executed scheme as it tends to have a cascading effect on many other development outcomes. Laden by huge populations with low literacy levels and wide spread poverty, in many developing countries several projects have shown partial success or none due to poor access to finance. The question of financial inclusion being central to the success of development initiatives is beyond reasonable doubt.

Concept of Financial Inclusion

The definition and concept of financial inclusion is broad and inclusive in nature; however, it has certain common features across the definitions which are the imminent pillars of the concept. Some significant definitions are discussed in this section.

World Bank describes financial inclusion as individuals and businesses have access to and use affordable financial products and services that meet their needs, which are delivered in a responsible and sustainable way. It is strongly believed that financial inclusion is a catalyst for achieving seven of the 17 Sustainable Development Goals (SDGs) (World Bank Group 2024).

The RBI states that Financial Inclusion is the process of ensuring access to appropriate financial products and services needed by all sections of the society in general and vulnerable groups such as weaker sections and low-income groups in particular at an affordable cost in a fair and transparent manner by mainstream institutional players. It can be observed how RBI puts great emphasis on not only providing access at affordable rates and in a transparent manner but the major idea is to have mainstream financial institutions getting to offer these services without discrimination to vulnerable sections of the society. This will help to create a very healthy landscape for financial inclusion in our country. Another definition also on similar lines says financial inclusion means that all people and businesses have access to – and are empowered to use- affordable, responsible financial services that meet their needs. These services include payments, savings credit and insurance (CGAP 2024). Most definitions emphasise on supply side factors of financial inclusion that is to provide easy and affordable access to financial services. In India, the Rangarajan Committee on Financial Inclusion (2008) defined Financial Inclusion as the process of ensuring access to financial services, timely and adequate credit for vulnerable groups such as weaker sections and low-income groups at an affordable cost. The Mohanty Committee on Medium-Term Path to Financial Inclusion (2015) suggested financial inclusion as providing convenient access to a basket of basic formal financial products and services that should include savings, remittance, credit, government-supported insurance and pension products to small and marginal farmers and low-income households at reasonable cost with adequate protection progressively supplemented by social cash transfers, besides increasing the access of small and marginal enterprises to formal finance with a greater reliance on technology to cut costs and improve service delivery. The focus of all definitions is to provide access to the underserved populations or organisations and promoting usage of affordable financial services. This emphasis and support of governments and institutions to the phenomenon of financial inclusion strongly targets inclusive growth in economies.

Causes of Financial Exclusion in India

There are so many economic, social, cultural, technological reasons that lead to a situation of financial exclusion. It differs in scale and gravity from country to country. Hence, it is important to look into these reasons before planning schemes and interventions for eliminating financial inclusion. The common reasons for India have been discussed in this section based on approach paper on National Strategy for Financial Inclusion 2019–24.

Lack of Surplus Income

This is one common reason why a large population does not find it necessary to open a basic savings bank account since they might if any have very negligible surplus incomes. This also discourages financial institutions to extend credit services to such populations as the risk involved would be very high. India was predominantly an agricultural nation made up of villages. The average land holding of a significant proportion of Indian farmers was small and marginal and this resulted in lack of assistance of advanced technologies for farming depriving them of good yields and additionally lack of high margins for their meagre yields. Now, the work ecosystems are changing and there is a clear shift of labour force towards services industry and rising numbers of middle-income group families, improving the levels of surplus incomes in the hands of people. However, there are still many vulnerable communities and populations with meagre disposable incomes which is still causing exclusionary trends that need to be dealt cautiously.

Not Suitable to Customer Requirements

The existing formats of conventional financial institutions did not address the requirements of many customers on the fringes of financial exclusion. Standard attempts to include them in the formal financial system were not finding success since many of them did not have steady cashflows that was a pre-condition to approving loans as otherwise systematic repayment of loan would be a problem. To a large extent microfinance institutions which came in strongly in the first decade of the new millennium addressed this gap and designed customised financial products with the liberal support of the regulators back then. This momentum did bring in a large number of excluded into the forefront of formal financial system.

Lack of Requisite Documents

Like the above discussion, exclusion of populations was also rampant due to lack of requisite documents required by the formal financial institutions, failing which there was no choice left but to lean back to the informal money lenders who would be many a times exploitative and charged exorbitant interest rates for financial assistance provided. Post the modern telephony systems and the Aadhar card mandates, it was much easier for formal financial institutions to lend to excluded populations or at least to open up a basic savings account through the Jan Dhan account. This happened in the second decade of the new millennium, in the meanwhile MFIs did pitch in strongly through SHGs and JLGs to extend group-based lending services. This made a leap change in the approach of the excluded populations and their need to be with the formal financial system.

Lack of Awareness about Products

There is a huge lack in awareness about the range of financial products like credits, insurance, pensions, fund remittances etc. not only among the lower income group populations but also the others in middle and high-income group populations. Financial literacy has not been taken up as a priority by household units and therefore, they continue to save and invest in the same set patterns as their previous generations would have advised. There has been a gradual change in this scenario with periodic inputs and awareness camps organised by financial institutions and much of grants from the government ministries. This factor has recently played a very crucial role in improving the scores of the financial inclusion index in the recent years.

Lack of Trust in the System

It has also been observed that large populations that were excluded have also had lacked confidence in the institutions offering financial services. This may be partly due to some scams that have eroded savings of their known ones or due to lack of awareness about their rights too. Regulators have put in much efforts these days to see that people are aware about their rights, money transactions and grievance redressal mechanisms. This plus increasing levels of literacy have helped to regain trust of the excluded populations who by choice stayed away from formal financial systems and banked with informal lenders who were in greater proximity with them.

High Transaction Costs

Most formal financial institutions offering conventional financial services were unable to reach out to the poor and far off regions in the country primarily due to the high transaction costs. The amount involved per transaction and the volumes of it rendered it unfeasible for conventional banks to service many clients profitably and hence they were excluded. Gradually these transaction costs are dropping due to technology and other alternative remote connectivity solutions. This has given fillip to financial inclusion phenomenon in India.

Remoteness of Service Provider

With lesser branch connectivity in rural areas particularly, the service providers were not known to the prospective clients and this remoteness of service providers caused lack of confidence subsequently there is an exclusionary trend created in such areas. One is always confident to deal with people who are known more so in money matters.

Poor Quality of Services Rendered

There have been problems with the quality of services provided by formal financial institutions also particularly in the past. This was more so during the periods when banking was dominated by only nationalized banks whereas in the post liberalisation era there is stiff competition among the private players and the nationalized banks the service quality has improved manifold. Simply since any delay in service or inadequate service will be quickly addressed by any other efficient competitor. So gradually, it is found that service quality also in a very planned manner is improving and creating a very welcoming environment for transacting your finances.

Gradually the causes of financial exclusion have been addressed by the subsequent governments and contributed favourably in the journey of financial inclusion in India.

History and Progress in FI

Financial Inclusion movements started gaining greater momentum with government initiatives in India in the post-independence era since government realised the fact that without people being connected to them and each other economically it will be very difficult to improve the well-being for such a large developing (at that time struck down with poverty and trauma) country. Gradually, government came up with various schemes that could give access to various financial services. Initially post-offices in India also served as one very big network of financial services provider and as recently announced, India is again going back to the same model (proposed Budget 2025) offering the last mile connectivity.

Initially the focus was on channelizing credit to the neglected sectors of the economy and weaker sections of the population and therefore various initiatives like expansion of branch network, introduction of Priority Sector Lending (PSL), launch of Lead Bank Scheme, promotion of Self-Help Groups (SHGs), Joint Liability Groups (JLGs), implementation of Business Correspondents (BC) model, among others. Indian banking gained gradually with the brick-and-mortar branches complemented by the BC model (RBI 2021). It has been noted in many studies that the Business Correspondent (BC) Model of banking has been able to bring significantly large unbanked populations to formal channels of banking particularly due to the push through rapid technological advancements in low-cost biometric applications and wider provision of financial services in terms of core banking solutions (Chauhan, 2022). The National Strategy for Financial Inclusion report (2018) recommended that the objective of providing a basic bouquet of financial services can be achieved through designing and developing customised financial products by banks and ensuring efficient delivery of the same through leveraging of Fin-tech and BC networks. It was recommended that banks should strive for capacity building of their BCs so that they can be utilized for delivery of a wider range of financial products such as life/non-life insurance products, pension products, mutual funds etc.

A major revolution that gave boost to financial inclusion in India was the microfinance movement. National Bank for Agricultural and Rural Development (NABARD) had introduced the SHG-Bank Linkage programme (SBLP) in 1992, subsequently covering and connecting large rural areas in the country with microfinance services through self-help group lending models. This was also the time when Mohmmad Yunus had successfully pioneered and established microfinance in Bangladesh too. Hence, the wave was not only favourable in India or South Asia, the entire globe had accepted the potential of microfinance to be an effective development tool for financial inclusion. Though there were some adverse times around 2010 but microfinance had merits which kept the momentum going with some special support from RBI. Immediately after this period was launched the *Pradhanmantri Jan Dhan Yojana* (PMJDY) in 2014. This brought a sweeping change in the inclusion ecosystem as many opened accounts particularly attaching the payment of various government run welfare schemes through Direct Benefit Scheme left no option with many unbanked populations. Even demonetisation had a role to play in opening various JDY accounts albeit with a lot of pros and cons associated. Many other schemes like the Atal *Beema* Yojana (2015), Ayushman Bharat Yojana (2018) etc. have a great role in connecting the financially excluded.

It is exciting to witness the way mobile money transactions number per 1000 adults have steadily shown rise of manifold times whereas other traditional measures like bank branches and ATMs too have not shown considerable rise as would have been expected. The above table shows how mobile technology has help gain the kind of financial inclusion that was targeted in India.

Thus, the nation is steadily rising in terms of performance in financial inclusion banking on few favourable scenarios particularly technology.

Access and Use of Financial Services

Indicator	*2013*	*2014*	*2015*	*2016*	*2017*	*2018*	*2019*	*2020*	*2021*	*2022*
Automated Teller Machines (ATMs) per 100,000 adults	12.87	17.80	19.70	21.24	22	21.65	20.95	21.50	21.21	24.64
Branches of commercial banks per 100,000 adults	11.85	12.87	13.54	14.06	14.51	14.50	14.58	14.74	14.42	14.31
Deposit accounts with commercial banks per 1,000 adults	1,160.72	1,337.41	1,541.79	1,731.27	1,881.54	1,937.25	1,967.61	2,030.71	2023.67	2130.48
Loan accounts with commercial banks per 1,000 adults	141.18	149.78	152.78	168.75	175.81	197.34	228.80	264.13	285.22	303.1
Mobile money transactions: number per 1,000 adults	35.98	116.06	270.11	627.69	1662.40	3031.52	4078.93	4111.97	3822.87	5008.21

IMF 'Financial Access Survey' 2023 - India statistics.

India's FI Standing Globally

Around the world, two billion people do not have access to financial products, such as a current account. In particular, large groups of poor people are excluded from financial services, either because there are no banks in their area or because banks do not consider them creditworthy. Financial inclusion therefore means that these people are given access (Doeveren v M, 2017). India introduced the Jan Dhan account (PMJDY), digital biometric identity card (Aadhaar) plus greater penetration to Mobile services and this triad (JAM) gave an ecosystem that infused a great leverage for financial inclusion and many initiatives have been taken to universalise digital payments in a convenient, safe, secure, transparent and affordable manner (RBI Bulletin, 2021). Digitization of finance has helped Indian Financial Inclusion agenda a great deal. An IMF paper puts forward this in a very succinct manner stating that India's FI journey has taught the developing countries many lessons. It recommends that a foundational approach providing a range of public infrastructure and policies can allow for significant synergies across different parts of the digital economy. Additionally, interoperability would be a useful tool for fostering competition in digital financial services plus a level playing field for data flows is necessary to ensure fair competition (Swallow *et al.*, 2021).

The chart 1.1 displays IMF Financial Access Survey's outcome based on the weighted average by region for economies whose data are available for 2019–2023 (some limitations of the data apply as a caveat). It is clearly evident that advanced economies, emerging and developing Europe, Latin America and Caribbean regions have secured financial inclusion by promoting access to finance through advancement in traditional methods of ATMs and bank branches, while Middle East and Central Asia and Sub-Saharan Africa regions have depended more on non-traditional methods for delivering financial access. It is the Emerging and Developing Asia region (including India) that has gone all out with both traditional as well as non-traditional methods of mobile money agents (registered) and retail agents to gain mileage with the goal of universal financial access (IMF Financial Access Survey, 2024).

Chart 1.1: Traditional and Non-traditional Access Points in Recent Years (2019 to 2023) (Number of Access Points Per 100,000 Adults)

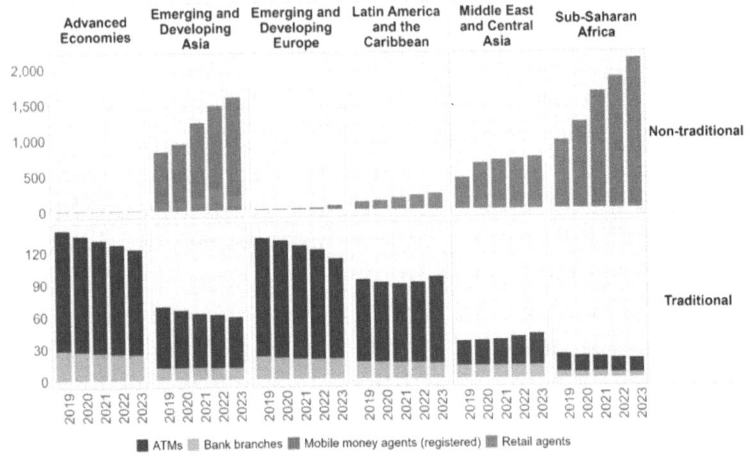

Source: Financial Access Survey and IMF staff calculations.

Construction and Results of RBI's FI Index

It is important to measure the progress attained towards the policy initiatives taken in the direction of financial inclusion. A multidimensional composite Financial Inclusion Index (FI-index) has been constructed based on 97 indicators which quantifies the extent of financial inclusion and is responsive to availability, ease of access, usage, unequal distribution and deficiency in services, financial literacy and consumer protection. The annual FI-Index with three sub-indices, Access, Usage and Quality measured on a scale of 0 to 100 stood at 53.9 in 2021 with Access as a subindex reflecting substantial progress in creating financial infrastructure in the country through combined efforts of all stakeholders (RBI Bulletin, 2021).

Backed by the awareness, infrastructure and robust security measures taken by the RBI along with partnering institutions and other stakeholders, the Financial Inclusion Index for India has consistently shown a rising trend. From 53.9 in 2021 to 56.4 in 2022, later 60.1 in 2023 and 64.2 in 2024, it has been indicating a steady increase. This signals a very favourable environment despite such a large population to be taken care of and moreover, being a country home to one of world's largest financially excluded populations. It is to be noted that the index used in here has also considered a 20 percent weightage for Quality as a parameter not just Access and Usage as in the case of many other countries. As discussed above in the section for causes of financial exclusion, building trust becomes a key corner stone of the pillar of financial inclusion. Many scams and fraudulent experiences of these vulnerable sections have contributed to the trust deficit towards the financial system. Hence, it was important that the system goes an extra mile to offer security in transactions and building greater trust in order for these sections of populations to use the elaborate infrastructure laid down for creating access and motivating usage. Therefore, the Financial Inclusion Index particularly reflects the efforts on awareness of financial services and overcoming psychological barriers by measuring effectiveness of grievance redressal mechanisms, consumer protection, inequality prevailing, financial literacy levels etc.

Chart 1.2: Financial Inclusion Index in India 2021–2024

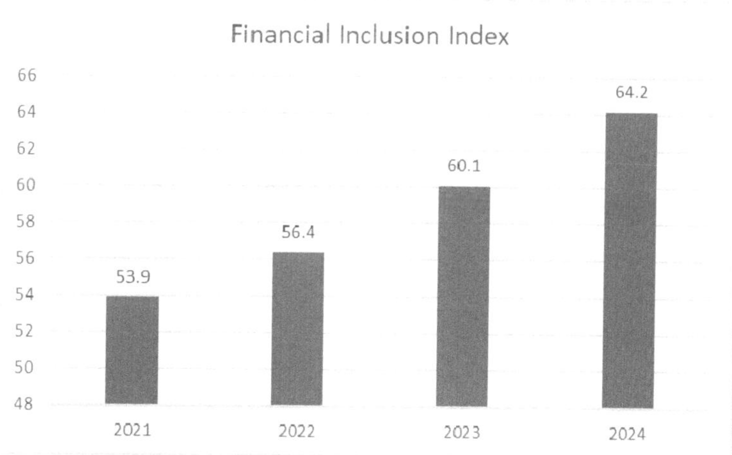

Source: RBI Bulletin.

Conclusion & Gap

The overall growth made in terms of parameters for financial inclusion by the country is immensely impressive and a lot of favourable scenarios are still favouring its growth. However, there are still some populations left out by current structures and they happen to be the most vulnerable communities like certain indigenous communities who do not want to join mainstream finance or many underprivileged women communities, certain lower caste denominations and certain professions that have reasons to be excluded by formal conventional financial service providers. One among such are females working as sex workers. This intersection of financial inclusion and women not associated with mainstream vocations and their vulnerabilities and difficulties is what is studied and presented in the following chapters.

CHAPTER 2

The Veil of Ignorance: An Introduction to the Study

Introduction

Inequalities of various kinds shroud our daily lives. However, it creates greater vulnerabilities for many who were already marginalised. This is what Capabilities Approach also suggests that it is possible to attain greater Functionings if there is a choice available and exercised towards enhancing the right capabilities (Sen, 1984 and Nussbaum, 2000). The role of institutions is also quite significant in this respect. The institutional theory considers that the various processes by which structures comprising of schemes, norms, rules, and routines, become established as authoritative guidelines for social behaviour (Richard, 2004). Different components of institutional theory explain how these elements are created, diffused, adopted, and adapted over space and time and how they may decline. Hence, the study focuses on the role of institutions with respect to sex work and workers that are an inseparable part of the society and yet ignored, consequently working and suffering quietly.

The current discussion is titled the veil of ignorance from two perspectives which are very contradicting from each other and yet applicable to the present study. The first approach is that the ignorance of people with respect to sex work makes it difficult for the sector to get formalised and acceptable in the society. So, it requires mass awareness through discussions in academic circles and other public discourses that will enable sex workers to function in this profession smoothly. The second aspect of 'veil of ignorance' is very much ingrained in sociological theory as advocated by John Rawls. He suggests that since situations and circumstances are different for every individual and groups, there is a difference in how people perceive and agree upon social contracts and how governing of work takes place. Therefore, one needs to sit behind the veil of ignorance so that we distance ourselves from our identity and then objectively analyse the situation for advocating policies for others particularly the disadvantaged groups to work with liberty (Rawls, 2001).

Various countries have different positions towards prostitution with respect to its legality. Around 69 countries prostitution is illegal, in 39 countries prostitution is restricted or having limited legality, it is legal in 54 countries and in 1 country there is no law for prostitution (World Population Review, 2025).

Chart 2.1: Countries where Prostitution is Legal 2025

Source: World Population Review, 2025.

The policy stands which various countries take on prostitution has been aptly summarised the World Population Review (2025) and presented in the following section:

- **Prohibitionism:** Prostitution is illegal (prohibited/criminalized) across the board. Selling, buying, organizing (via brothels, pimps, etc.), and soliciting sex for money are all against the law. This approach is common in deeply religious countries, especially countries that outlaw pornography.
- **Neo-abolitionism:** This philosophy considers prostitution to be violence against women. Selling sex is *technically* legal—but buying, organizing, and soliciting sex are all illegal. Prostitutes are considered legally blameless when caught in the act, but their clients and pimps (the prostitute's "organizer" or boss) are prosecuted. This "reverse loophole" is designed to suppress demand.

- **Abolitionism:** The most prevalent approach worldwide. Selling sex and buying sex are both legal. However, in an effort to prevent exploitation of the sex worker, public solicitation; the operation of brothels; and forms of "organization" such as pimping, procuring, and forced prostitution are all usually prohibited.
- **Legalization:** Selling, buying, and some forms of organizing (typically brothels) and soliciting of sex are legal. But they are also regulated, such as requiring prostitutes to register or only allowing prostitution in certain districts.
- **Decriminalization:** Selling, buying, organizing, and solicitation of sex are all legal (or simply not addressed in the law at all) and are subject to minimal or no special regulations.'

Table 2.1: Position of Select Countries on Prostitution

Country	*Legal Stand*	*Approach Used*	*Implication*
India	Limited Legality	Abolitionism	Prostitution is legal, brothels, solicitation and offering to sell sex in public place is illegal.
South Africa	Illegal	Prohibitionism	Still widespread
Germany	Legal	Legalisation	Organised and regulated.
Israel	Limited Legality	Neo-abotionalism	Selling is legal but buying, organising and solicitation is illegal.
United States	Legal/Illegal	Legalisation/ Prohibitionism	Legal in 49.5 countries. Only in some parts of Nevada it is still prohibited.

Source: Table drawn from Excerpt of World Population Review (2025).

In India, prostitution is not a criminal offense but soliciting prostitution and prostitution in a public place is illegal. If prostitution is legal then sex workers could be covered under social security schemes. There are more than 8.25 lakh identified sex workers in India [one can assume 10 percent to be male and remaining females] more than half of them are from five southern states Andhra Pradesh, Tamil Nadu, Karnataka, Kerala and Telangana (India Today, 2022). Though there could be other reasons of these states displaying higher numbers, as many times females in sex work do not want to come out and identify themselves as one [as it can be observed West Bengal has only claimed to be at 17,327, whereas at Sonagachi it has one of the oldest organised sex markets of Asia]. Hence, the number cannot be definitive, however, it can certainly be indicative of the rise in these numbers over a period of time and as they become huge in numbers coupled with being a sight of vulnerabilities, it is all the more important to engage into productive discussions about the well being of female sex workers and design and deliver meaningful social security schemes. A Constitution Bench of the Supreme Court on September 6, 2018 ruled that provisions of Section 377 of the IPC were unconstitutional as they infringed on the fundamental rights of autonomy, intimacy and identity of LGBTQIA+ community in India, hence the order identified prostitution as a profession and directed that sex workers be accorded a life of dignity and this decision might help to include a large number of people into the mainstream society.

Not many of them want to be in this trade by choice however there are some who are in the profession by their own choice too. Many interventions have been experimented with these women. Microfinance came like a ray of hope to many organisations and individuals. Several MFIs and other not-for-profit organisations tried to generate alternative means of livelihood for females who were into commercial sex work.

The inclusive approach of all welfare programmes in India have endeavoured to reach out to as many vulnerable communities as possible particularly through its micro lending activities. Government found success in different anti-poverty and other welfare programmes in India (NABARD, 2006). Microfinance has received great acceptance as a source of development finance in India. Aideyan (2009) found that households with access to such programs do have more substantial social and economic benefits than those without access. However, as we bring in the fore the most excluded communities like the Female Sex Workers (FSWs), there is not much work reported.

Chart 2.2: Figures on Prostitution in India

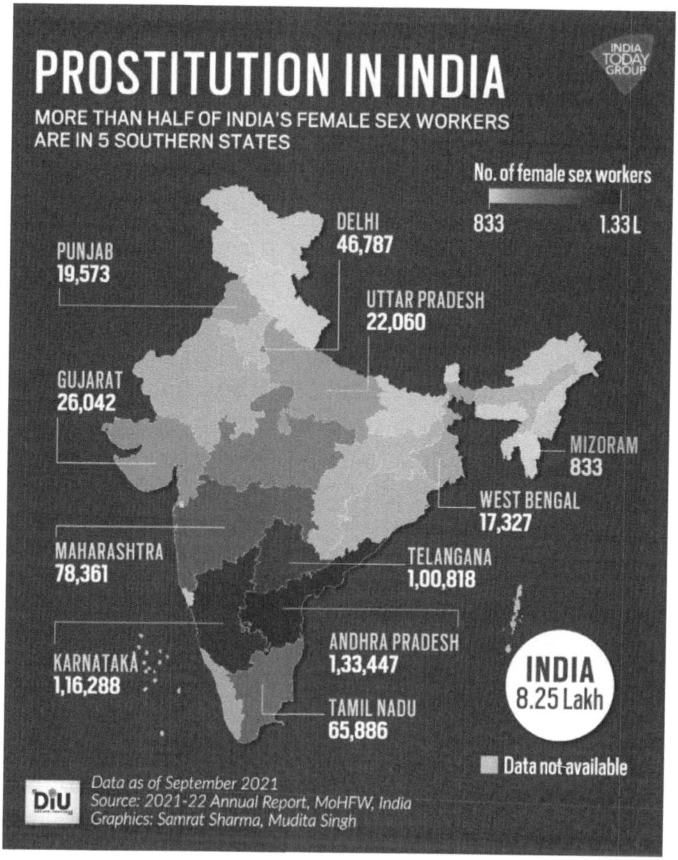

Source: India Today (2022).

Some initial observations in this area are that there are many cases of failures reported in such initiatives where the major reasons are lack of capacity building and proper group formation. There is still shortage of funding for MFIs/NGOs who are functioning in this area. There is a chance of many of them being subject to fraudulent finance schemes. Never the less, the priority should be to provide social and economic security (Fisher & Sriram, 2008). In India, major cities have pockets that have been occupied and noted as 'red light' areas which to some extent allows FSWs to organise themselves too. Some studies have also done in such cities regarding their social and economic conditions but not many studies have been done with Ahmedabad city in focus, hence it is important to study the city with respect to the condition of FSWs.

Objective of the Study

- To understand the role of Financial Inclusion and consequent vulnerabilities in individuals caused by lack of it.
- To understand the condition of Female sex workers in Ahmedabad district and access to finance and health services.
- To find out reasons that lead the Female sex workers into this means of livelihood.
- To investigate about initiatives taken by not-for-profit organisations and microfinance institutions in enhancing alternative livelihood opportunities.
- To recommend policy initiatives that ameliorate the conditions of Female Sex workers.

Literature Review

Indian constitution is probably one of the best texts written from the perspective of inclusive growth. Having strong emphasis on supporting all marginalised segments, it has special provisions to empower women in general (Article 14, 15, 39, 42, 46 etc.). The Constitution of India not only just grants equality to women but empowers the State to adopt measures of positive discrimination in favour of women for neutralizing the cumulative socio-economic, education and political disadvantages faced by women (Legal Service India-Web). India also has ratified various international conventions and human rights instruments committing to secure equal rights for women and the one of the most significant ones signed in 1993 being Convention of Elimination of All Forms of Discrimination Against Women (CEDAW). That is because typically women in India have been long marginalised and this has been seen historically, ethically, religiously and culturally too. However, there is need to provide specific support to Female Sex Workers (FSW) too by mentioning explicit reference to FSWs and support provided to them. Since there are so many development programmes being designed in India too but they do not use the term Sex worker explicitly and this renders them invisible while accounting for welfare payments that need to be made.

Hence, women are already a marginalised entity in India, female sex workers are even more an excluded segment among this marginalised entity due to the stigma attached to their profession.

The study is interested to find out whether any financial support for alternative livelihoods enhances the capability of FSWs to have better alternatives in life for their wellbeing. Literature supports that microfinance or lending in very small amounts has shown fabulous results in improving the economic condition of women and their families living below poverty line (Yunus, 1999). The prerequisites commonly found by various studies are cohesive group formation through common socio-economic background, capacity building support through external machinery, quick and easy access to microfinance products and services. All the aforesaid phenomena were also noted with FSWs, the beneficiary group under the current study but many do not get respite from poverty and hence their profession. Theorists and practitioners are often blinded by the overwhelming policy support, in India and internationally, and therefore simplistically assume that with an infusion of capital in the form of 'directed credit' or micro-credit to poor households, they will be able to break out of the vicious cycle of poverty (Fisher & Sriram, 2008).

With the help of NGOs many SHGs organised themselves into federations for performing non-financial functions like social and capacity building activities, promotion of SHGs, facilitate training of SHGs and their internal audit (RBI, 2018). These groups and institutions try and support FSWs in gaining economic empowerment and providing a choice of alternative livelihood. This access to having a choice is what is valued as a significant 'Capability' in the dimensions listed in Nussbaum's central list of functional capabilities for women (Nussbaum, 2000).

The government sponsored many programmes and projects to bring the excluded poor into the mainstream "development" however, many of these programmes failed to target the vulnerable poor. There is in fact a school of thought that believes that government assistance to the poor often creates dependency and disincentives that make consequences worse. Moreover, despite decades of aid, communities and families appear to be increasingly fractured, offering a fragile foundation on which to build (Morduch, 1999). This industry has evolved over the last two decades and reached over 25 per cent penetration level in the total addressable market, in 2019. The microfinance lenders aim to provide easy access to formal credit to customers that need it the most and would not typically be eligible for bank credit, thus providing inclusion for a large rural and urban population of the country. A vast majority of the borrowers constitute women who are just above the poverty line and striving to improve the living conditions of their household (KPMG, 2019).

The microfinance industry is highly heterogenous with a wide range of organisations operating under distinct legislative frameworks including banks, small finance banks, NBFCs, Not-for-Profit MFIs and NBFC-MFIs (Fatima, 2024). Hence, ideally it should be offering a wide range of products and serving a wide range of populations too. Microfinance institutions provide their clients with variety of financial products such as microloans, micro-savings and microinsurance. These products aid in the development of a savings culture, the provision of working capital to small businesses, and the protection against financial shocks. Microfinance institutions have also implemented novel models such as mobile banking and digital payments in order to reach more people (Pant, 2018). Ozili, P.K. and Syed A.A. (2024) find that the major determinants of financial inclusion in India are income, age, gender, education, employment, ICT, bank branch network and nearness to a bank. They state that some criticisms of the financial inclusion efforts in India include the inability to meet the specific needs of the poor, poor geographical access, excessive transaction cost, inappropriate banking products, financial illiteracy and a large digital divide between tech savvy and non-tech savvy people. A bibliometric study done by Lwesya and Mwakalobo (2023) emphasised in their work on a cluster of studies that found that despite the positive impact of MFIs, the saturation of uncoordinated microfinance institutions and the expansion of multiple indebtedness have created challenges for regulators and management of microfinance institutions, leading to deterioration in loan portfolios and the financial sustainability of institutions. Hence, the role of the regulators is greater than ever imagined.

Meki and Quinn (2024) suggest that despite a lack of evidence for transformational effects, many people continued to use microfinance, underscoring the significance of basic financial services in people's lives. The academic and policy debate has thus moved from '*does* microfinance work?' to '*for whom* does it work, *how* does it work, and how can it be made to *work better*?'. Therefore, it has been well understood and accepted now that microfinance cannot be the panacea to all problems but to some very specialised ones it can do wonders. The need is to identify for whom does it work right and how.

Raccanello, K, Anand, J, and Santos, A.V. (2011) bring out an insightful connect on how gender-asset-ownership is related to women's participation in informal finance schemes. Using a random sample of 250 women from Puebla, Mexico, their probit model estimates revealed that younger women with intermediate level of education are more likely to access the informal finance sector. Khursheed, Ambreen (2022) in an empirical study provides valuable insights into the efforts made by an MFI in Pakistan to empower women and combat poverty by encouraging women's entrepreneurship. This paper not only examines empowerment which women are attaining from microfinance but also assists MFIs to know about their significance in developing the economy. Pattnaik, D., Ray, Sougata and Hassan, K.M. (2024) conducted a bibliometric analysis on 1599 studies published between 1987 to 2022 and found that a significant portion of microfinance literature focuses on the impact of microfinance institutions (MFIs) on clients, encompassing social and financial dimensions affecting enterprises, households, and communities. indicate increased household consumption, non-land assets, and improved education, particularly for girls. Thus, working on women of the household for development purposes has always given positive results and the current study also therefore continues to check why females in sex work could or could not benefit with microfinance initiatives as claimed by so many studies.

There are many thoughts doing rounds as to why women enter sex work, whether by force or by choice. The historic assumption is that they are into this trade by force and not by choice. Times are changing and therefore it becomes even more pertinent to check out whether women in sex work have to real autonomy and choice to chose any other work or sex work as per their own free will. Boroumandfar, Z., Esmaeili, R. and Mohaghegh, N. (2022) in their study on female sex workers bring out what the participants in Iran sensed of "what pushed me into sex worker" which included the five main categories of despair, psychic restlessness, getting drunk by alcohol and drug, incomplete families, not to be left behind by the sudden social changes. Potter, K., Martin, J. and Romans, S. (1999) found in an experimental study about intervention of MFI that sex workers' families were of lower socioeconomic status and had experienced more parental separation than did those with the NGO women. The mothers of sex workers were more frequently the family's main wage earner. Sex workers described both parents as less caring than did the women connected with NGO. They were significantly more likely than the NGO women to report childhood sexual abuse. The sex workers were more likely to have left home early, to have become pregnant before the age of 19 years and to not have completed tertiary study. These findings are significant in understanding how MFIs can make a difference to the lives of female sex workers if the development projects are designed appropriately. Jewkes, R., Milovanovic, M., Otwombe, K., Hlongwane, K., Hill, N., Mbowane, V., ... Coetzee, J. (2023) conducted a study using structural equation modelling of the South African National Sex Worker Survey by enrolling 3005 women in sex work using multistage sampling across all South Africa's provinces to get insights on sex work stigma, its drivers and their interrelation. It was found that experience of external/enacted and internalised stigma was widespread. Non-partner rape, intimate partner violence and partner controlling behaviour compounded internalised stigma. They strongly recommended that "reducing sex workers' exposure to external/enacted stigmatising behaviour, including by enabling more to work indoors, and providing greater protection from partner violence and rape, are critical for better health and well-being. Ending the criminalisation of sex work is foundational for safer working conditions and better health outcomes for sex workers, similarly providing adequately funded mental and physical health and social care through sex work specific programmes". Miles, G.M. *et al.* (2020) state there are dependency structures within massage parlours and with their families seem to play a key role in the life situations that can be positive or negative or both. One of the research studies conducted in Nigeria which surveyed several interventions pointed out on limitations like funding, absence of grass-roots engagement, dearth of appropriate professionals, corruption, weak political will etc (Agwu et al. 2020). A study carried out by Pachauri, S., Pachauri, A., Mittal, K. (2022) revealed that women in sex work faced mental health problems and were ill-treated and abused by the community, police, and others. The participants made statements like, "We are sexually abused by the police and other men around us. They do not pay us after sexual intercourse and sometimes they bring 4–5 men with them to abuse us". "If we have to get abused anyway, we might as well earn through sex work". Therefore, they actively chose sex work because they found more perks in sex work than in other jobs. They faced stigma in society which resulted in mental depression and isolation. All the above literatures suggest strongly towards having more deeper and wider research studies to be done in the area of female sex workers' autonomy.

There are few works that have been done in this area particularly in Ahmedabad city. The current study tries to address this gap in literature.

Research Methodology

The research methodology for the study had to be very carefully thought through since not much has been published and secondly, getting good quality and accurate data was challenging.

Data Collection

The study included primary as well as secondary data study. Secondary study will rely on journals, books, newspapers and reports carrying researches with the said topic. Not much has been published from the social science perspective. Though there have been some reports and much being done from a medical perspective in this area. Other data where the study depended on secondary data is the historic and demographical aspects of Ahmedabad city.

- **Primary Survey:** A survey was undertaken with the help of not-for-profit organisations (including academic institutions) which are functioning in the sector with similar objectives for data collection. Survey of FSWs was undertaken through a CBO. Since it was a detailed qualitative study, data was collected from ten FSWs. Informed consent was taken from all respondents and the information so collected will be kept confidential and used only for academic purposes. Major and significant data has been collected from experts who have worked in this area for many years. A panel discussion was conducted in this regard since it provides deep insights from the experiences of the experts and especially when one is dealing with lack of published data in the chosen area. The data collection was primarily conducted through direct interviews for qualitative data.
- **Sample frame and sampling method:** Primarily FSW beneficiaries who have received systematic institutional support – monetary or non-monetary. Sample will consist of respondents who have in past or at present been a FSW and a member of MF or not-for- profit institutions providing support. The type of sampling used is purposive. Since there is no concrete Universe available particularly in Ahmedabad district as FSWs are scattered and not organised, snow-ball sampling method was undertaken for the purpose of identifying sample with the help of the CBO of FSWs working in Ahmedabad.
- **Research Design:** The analysis will be largely qualitative in nature. This helps to describe many complex situations and influences that are difficult to capture in quantitative studies the research design of the study was exploratory in nature.
- **Limitations:** The study has relied on the information shared by the institutions assuming it to be true and analysis is based on this information. This certainly carries the risk of data being manipulated which investigator will try to triangulate and verify as far as possible. The Census of India also does not give any information on FSWs functioning in different regions and neither are there any much good surveys available, so whatever data has been made available through the CBO is taken to be the most authentic data and this can have its

own limitations as many women may not be still associated with the CBO but since they are scattered and unidentifiable, the method of data collection chosen was to contact FSWs through the CBO only.

Expected Outcomes

Also, the prime take-away from the project is the enriching discussions with the stakeholders working actively and contributing in the sector. This will help enhance class room discussions for all academics and for further research.

Chapter Layout

The chapters have been lined up in a way to get the perspective on significant concepts and progress in financial inclusion in India in the first chapter and in the latter chapters, discussions on concepts and frameworks and then understanding the conditions of FSWs in Ahmedabad.

1. Financial Inclusion in India—A Progressive Story
2. The Veil of Ignorance- An Introduction to the Study
3. Sex Work and its Perils
4. FSWs in Ahmedabad
5. Role of Institutions for the FSWs
6. Conclusion and Recommendations

CHAPTER 3

Sex Work and its Perils

Understanding Sex Work

Sex work is one of the oldest professions in the world. However, the taboo around it is so entrenched that no one wants to openly have deliberations on it. Therefore, the awareness for this profession remains largely very low barring sex workers themselves, some medical practitioners, police departments, NGOs working for their welfare and customers soliciting commercial sex. The fact that sex work has always been legal in India is also not known to many[1]. This can be majorly attributed to the fact that it is not encouraged to discuss such matters in public and whatever little is known is the idea that one forms from various media particularly movies which are more often than not reprimanding sex work and paint a repugnant picture of sex workers.

The UNDP refers to sex work as a contractual arrangement where sexual services are negotiated between consenting adults with the terms of engagement agreed upon between the seller and the buyer (UNDP, 2012). It has been accepted as a work format for livelihood if the seller is freely willing to engage in the work. If it is not consensual and there is no free will then it could amount to trafficking. However, since there are not many discussions and awareness on this issue, sex work continues to be believed as unlawful and people engaged in it are treated as outlaws, undignified and immoral. Resultantly, there is a lot of vulnerability that accrues around sex work and workers. The next section discusses the perils of sex work that such vulnerabilities create and the need of welfare provisions particularly for women engaged in sex work.

---

[1] Sex work is legal in India. Pimping or trafficking for sex work is criminal and a punishable offence.

Gender in Sex Work

Gender is a term that comes into question more so when the term sex also is discussed. Though the current study investigates the condition of women in sex work, it is well understood that there are other genders also involved in sex work. The condition of even other genders in sex work is quite pathetic because men and transgenders also face an equally challenging environment in the sex industry if not more. The CBO that the study got associated also was actively functioning for the welfare of MSW segment too. There is a clear need to do much more in organising the sex work industry. The recent Supreme Court Judgement will have a great impact on the future of the sex workers industry but the present remains bleak since no one wants to come out and share their identities. Women particularly are the marginalised sections and FSWs among them are even more cornered and a non-entity for the policy makers. And this adds to the perils of women in sex work. MBonye, M *et al.* (2012) stated that gender inequity is manifested in the social and economic burden women carry in relation to men and that women's experiences of different stages from childhood to adult life have a role to lead them to sex work due to their specific gender relations.

Perils of Sex Work

Though the current study only focuses on female sex workers, sex work basically is being carried out by all genders- males, females and transgenders. Exploitation and risks of males and transgenders are also very many whiles being engaged in the profession. But it will be beyond the scope of the study to currently discuss them though the nature of perils more or less remains similar.

Physical Health

Sex work is extremely physically involving and therefore exhausting. The work-life, therefore remains short-lived until the physical health permits the worker. The most common ailment that Female Sex Workers contract would be the sexually transmitted diseases which cause vaginal discharge, ulcers, pain in the abdomen and painful sexual intercourse (Department for

International Development Report, 2004). 'The standards of practice in prevention and cure regarding sexual health issues vary widely. The sex workers from the upper income category (eg. call girls) are better informed, take precautions more often (and could also be getting treated early enough and through a competent specialist)' (DFID Report, 1999). This report which was presented to Ahmedabad Aids Control Society, strongly recommends intensively addressing STD services among the sex workers. Apart from the these there are regular other health issues that FSWs would face but there is a tendency of avoidance to get treatment which generally has disastrous impacts on their bodily well-being. Many international researches also support that there is stigma in the society that dissuades FSWs to openly go out and seek medical help and this creates greater dependency and vulnerability as their physical health deteriorates. Hence, it is quintessential that any policy takes care of providing affordable and good medical services to FSWs.

Mental Health and Well-Being

Along with physical health, mental health and well-being is a facet of health that is most ignored among the sex workers. The exploitation and violence that many face quietly due to the secret shroud around the profession leads to many kinds of mental health issues, most of which assumably go unreported. But it is not shocking considering that many women do not even report about their physical health conditions, mental health and well-being is largely ignored among the mainstream in India so it will remain so for female sex workers if timely corrective actions are not taken. Many undergo depression, loneliness, fear psychosis etc. due to the treatments that are meted out by clients and society at large.

Violence at Work

Many a times violence is resorted to by clients meeting female sex workers. It may not be a regular feature at work but certainly episodically it is not uncommon to come across such instances. In such circumstances, it becomes very difficult for FSWs to manage their affairs and the client and it harms them in many ways including loss of work till they heal. It is difficult for them to work and sometimes they lose their will to work. Most women in sex work do not resort to police as the police (mostly men) also view it as something that they deserve as they chose to work in this profession. Therefore, it is more important to underscore the significance of decriminalisation of sex work and removing the stigma around it. Violence against women in general and particularly women in sex work should not be tolerated. This will help building capabilities of women by guiding them to chose their professions with free will.

Other Exploitations

It is not uncommon to find exploitation in this profession particularly from unruly clients. This would be more if there are intermediaries between the buyer and seller. Of course, trafficking being another extreme of such exploitations. Women and children being trafficked for sex work is one of the greatest crimes increasing at very fast pace across the world. These crimes are directly addressed within the law-and-order system. Moreover, there are innumerable unacknowledged and unreported instances of exploitation particularly of less payments made, time and travel issues. Earlier there were issues of the police being insensitive too but now due to a lot of reforms and training within police department, there is a marked change in how police view and support the women who are genuine and dependent on sex work for their livelihood.

Societal Pressures

The society at large still does not perceive sex work as a profession and this renders a lot of adversities for females in the profession. There is no proper place for offering services and working systematically for a large majority of FSWs. Subsequently, they face a lot of wrath in the streets. Or if one tries and starts in a residential society, one will be forced to vacate the location due to the stigma attached with the work. Hence, if state openly supports those women who have chosen to be in the profession and provide them organised and protected spaces for the pursuing the profession, it is safe from societal stigma and also other exploitative hands.

Family

Contrary to the expectations of the majority, many women who are in sex work operate with the support of their families. However, many-a-times, it is only the husband of the family who is aware of the actual profession of the FSW but not the other members of the family. So, one always risks this divulgence of information and continuously is under this pressure of mysteriously carrying on a profession. It is saddening to find that the efforts of women who struggle to keep their family going with the incomes that they earn by pursuing such a perilous profession often get unnoticed by their family members also. Thus, getting support in their grey days of ill-health and old age is also not a surety. Still most FSWs are happy working for their families and seeing them prosper despite whatever they go through. When their kids get proper education and are able to take up professions of their choice and find a good reputed position in society, FSWs admit to have found great satisfaction.

Cost

The profession is more lucrative than many other mainstream livelihood options and therefore many continue it for a lifetime. However, one has to spend a fortune to maintain the standards and be in the profession specially among the upper income strata of sex workers. More so, for their health purposes, FSWs do need to spend a fortune if there are treatments to be taken. The high costs would therefore include health cost primarily, then expenses meted out for a particular appearance to be attained to be in the profession, traveling costs if there is no fixed location available, hotel/lodge room rents which can be hefty depending on the extent of criminalisation of the act and the stigma prevailing in the area regarding the profession, sometimes hefty bribes to be paid etc. So, earnings come with greater costs which sometimes they themselves are not well-informed about.

Conclusion

Sex work is a very risky profession and so all the workers associated with it are categorised as high-risk workers. Therefore, it becomes all the more necessary to understand, evaluate and support the sex work profession and workers involved in it through various measures.

CHAPTER 4

Female Sex Workers in Ahmedabad

Introduction

The city in which the study was conducted is Ahmedabad, located in the western region of India. It is very important to know the historical context of the city in order to understand with the condition of female sex workers in Ahmedabad.

Ahmedabad was founded by Sultan Ahmed Shah of Gujarat dynasty in 1411 AD on the banks of river Sabarmati. The city was located close to the trading town of Asawal, founded by a tribal Asha Bhil in 11th century. During British rule, it was an important centre for freedom struggle because of Mahatma Gandhiji's active participation. It was also known as 'Manchester of India' for its rich and diverse flourishing textile industry. It has now grown to a metropolis of more than 5 million people and is the largest city of Gujarat state. The city is a known centre for industrial and commercial activities. In 1986, the municipal area of the city was expanded to 98.15 sq. km. The new areas are developing fast and are being gradually provided with all civic amenities and infrastructural facilities. As per 2011 census, the population of city of Ahmedabad is 5577940. The density of the population is 9900 per square km. and the sex ratio is 898 females per 1000 males. The percentage of the scheduled castes and tribes in total population is 13.7% and 0.8% respectively.

Apart from the well-known mammoth textile mills, other industries like chemicals, iron and steel, machine tools, machine spare parts, pharmaceuticals, small scale and cottage industries had also come up in the city both in organised and unorganised sector.

The number of various small and big registered factories in 1989 was 3256 and the average number of workers working in these factories was 202,089 (statistical outline of Ahmedabad city 1991). Ahmedabad's population increased to 5,577,940 in 2011 from 4,519,000 in 2001, a jump of 23.43% (it has been long since Census and so figures will be much higher now). As per Census 2011, the majority of migrants to Ahmedabad came from Rajasthan (2.16 lakh), followed by UP (1.9 lakh) and Maharashtra (1.10 lakh). Within India, a large portion of the 21 crore migrants in 2011 were intra-state migrants (88%), while inter-state migration comprised about 12%.

The city has a predominantly Hindu population (81.56%) Muslims (13.51%), Jains, Christians, and Sikhs form 3.62%, 0.85% and 0.24 percent respectively. Gujarati is the mother tongue of a vast majority of the population. The other important languages spoken by the people are Urdu, Hindi, Marathi, Marvadi, Sindhi etc.

The city of Ahmedabad was 5,52,162 dwelling units of which 91,121 units are situated in 1023 slums having an estimated population of 4,79,029 people. The city has 1409 chawls with 1,36,773 dwelling units and an estimated population of 8,11,220 people. The population of slums and chawls put together is 12,90,249 or 41.3% of the population of the city.

The total number of slums in Ahmedabad City are 51,451 which is home to almost 2,50,681 residents. This constitutes approximately 4.49% of the total population of the city. This is the most disadvantaged group of the city of Ahmedabad and need special care and attention. Information about demographic and health characteristics revealed that the average number of persons in a city household is 5.54 and the birth rate is 30.99. There are four general hospitals in the city, 1851 beds are in municipal hospitals. The growth of the city, migration of male labourers and its socio-economic implications have changed the traditional relationships in the city.

FSWs in Ahmedabad

Around 1930s when Ahmedabad city was known to be the Manchester of India due to the flourishing textile mills in the city, approximately 30 percent of the labour engaged in these factories were women. Such was the progressiveness that one could observe in the Gujarati society of those times regarding the economic empowerment of women. However, as mechanisation of processes began in the mills, layoffs were inevitable and apparently those families from which both husband and the wife were working, the wives were laid off. Subsequently the number of women in the workforce in organised and formal employment fell drastically and some statistics say it was less than 1 percent then. This pushed the women to take up alternative livelihoods which were rare, unsustainable and subject to exploitative conditions.

In 1980s when the mills were closing down one by one in this once progressive city, the labour force was largely male dominated. Hence, when the lay-offs happened consequent to the mills shutting down, the males of the families in the city did not have any much opportunity to work nor the skill-sets or know-how to create or grab other livelihood opportunities in such large numbers. Some 52 textile mills out of a total of 86 have been closed, as a result of which nearly 50,000 textile mill workers had been rendered unemployed.

This was a period of great economic crisis and every labourer family in the city and in many nearby towns were not able to fend for themselves and their families. There were health emergencies too in their homes. Subsequently, many women from these households took up to sex work and it was normally with the consent of the husband and marital family. Left with no choices, these women took up to a profession that they had never much heard of and surely going to change their lives forever.

In the present times, there are approximately ten thousand [rough estimation] Female Sex Workers in Ahmedabad city operating from several places. An old estimate that is available is that they operate from more than 47 different locations of the city. These comprised of 23 locations in industrial areas, 6 in the Old city and 18 in the Western Ahmedabad (Jani *et al.*, 1999. Ahmedabad AIDS Control Society Report).

The sex workers in the city can be categorised into the following:

1. Street workers
2. Call girls
3. Residential
4. Brothel

5. Guest house
6. Others (e.g. Mobile sex workers)

Street Sex Workers

Street workers are the poorest among the sex workers. They are seen around bus stations, railway stations, and other areas where many people pass by. They establish contact with their customers directly or through rickshaw driver for which he gets a small commission of 5–10 rupees. The customer is usually taken to some guest house for sex. Guest houses are small lodge like houses with 4-6 rooms and are let out to travellers for low tariffs. Guest houses are seen in areas like railway station and other areas where general public movement is high. Street workers are distributed in various points of industrial area and stay mainly in the nearby villages. Street workers charge anywhere between 40–200 rupees per act of sex. Though the auto rickshaw driver often acts as a broker, he or other people in her close environment do not have a significant control over her. The general health status of the street workers appears to be poor. Condom use is gradually increasing and if STDs occur are not properly treated. Though there are occasional police arrests there does not seem to be significant harassment. After the arrest, the street worker is produced in the court and is usually fined some nominal amount (Jani *et al.*, 1999. Ahmedabad AIDS Control Society Report).

Call Girls

Call girls come from within the city and also from other towns/ cities. These places may be within the state or outside the state like Delhi, Bombay and Bengal. Majority of the live in Western Ahmedabad and Old city. Call girls operate through a system of brokers (*dalals).* These may be simple or it may be a complex procedure involving different stages of clearances to assure safety. Many different systems of operations are involved. The brokers get roughly 10 to 25% of the call girl's earnings. Call girls charge between 1000–25000. If the client is regular and is trusted, he will be permitted to meet the call girl directly. Such trusted clients often introduce other clients also. The call girls are constantly in touch with their brokers through telephone/

pager/cell phone. The clients for the call girls belong to the city but some of them are also business travellers, non-resident Indians (NRIs) and politicians. Due to the connections that some call girls have they gradually gather considerable power.

Residential

In this type of operation one sex worker works from an apartment or a house. She may have others staying with her who may or may not know of her involvement in sex work (e.g. In houses where all the adults go out for work). Usually, sex workers in this category entertain only very trusted clients and new clients come through client-to-client work. Brokers do not appear to have a role here. It is very difficult to study this sector due to the confidentiality maintained around it.

Brothels

There are scores of brothels in the city. Brothel is a house where 3 to 5 sex workers stay and sell sex. There are no large-scale brothels in the city as found in Mumbai and Calcutta. Most of the brothels were in Western Ahmedabad were in affluent areas operating from apartments in flats whereas the brothels in peri urban areas were in slums. The customers in this category are regulars and those brought by rickshaw drivers. Brothels are usually managed by one elderly or middle-aged lady. The fee charged by sex workers in brothels range from Rs. 50–5000. The sum brothels generally charge on the lower side and the residential area brothels charge on higher side. The health care also reflects the socio-economic disparity between the two.

Guest Houses

Guest houses provide place for sex as mentioned above. In addition to this in certain guest houses the personnel working there will also arrangements for the sex worker if the inmate so desires. Guest houses are in touch with sex workers and can access them when needed. Thus, guest houses operate to liaison for both, providing the location and providing the sex worker too.

Based on the survey conducted during the course of the current study, it was found that most women were into this profession due to severe financial crisis at homes. This was also corroborated by our sector expert, Prof. Gaurang Jani, who said that not only was the mill closure a major blow to the household economies of Ahmedabad city but also the early 1990s stock market crisis, popularly known as Harshad Mehta scam also had adversely affected the financial conditions of homes in and around Ahmedabad and this resulted in many women getting into sex work to fulfil the needs of their families.

Many women have accepted the fact that this profession is better than many other, in the sense that most other professions that they have engaged in earlier also exploited them badly, at least their monetary needs are fulfilled in this profession. These groups are vulnerable and when crisis hits, their vulnerability and helplessness only increases hence most FSWs have openly admitted that it is not so easy to leave this profession as there is good money that they can earn and in these times of inflation, by force they keep some loyal clients who are like 'ATMs' for them as they financially support these women during any financial difficulties that they face. This is unlikely of other professions.

However, women in this profession are hopeful for the next generation of theirs in terms of their children, that they may study well and prosper. And this is happening because, many women who were interviewed under the study have informed that, their children have been doing well and settled in much more acceptable professions and so their children will not have to undergo the difficulties that they themselves have faced. So, if one asks FSWs in general one thing needed by them, then the answer is respect and the other is good education for their children.

FSWs in Other Cities

Female sex workers have been a population group excluded very conveniently by the society, to the extent that they are treated invisible by many policies as well. It is a pitiable condition how we reduce the rights of an equal citizen to someone who is bound to be doomed because of the profession which she most often than not is forced to take up due to her circumstances at home, to save her family from dire consequences of poverty and deprivation. This is also due to largely a robust patriarchal system that exists around women in India which does not allow her to pursue higher education and often not allowed to pursue a career from the very beginning quoting marital reasons. However, the contradiction that surfaces, as one interviews many female sex workers, is that her marital family has been instrumental in her getting into this profession of sex work (sometimes of course her maiden family too) and secondly, she lacked any capabilities to take up a good career option rewarding her enough to take care of her family. So then, is society getting their ill-informed biases to build strong stereotypes for female sex workers?

Various countries have different positions towards prostitution with respect to its legality. Around 69 countries prostitution is illegal, in 39 countries prostitution is restricted or having limited legality, it is legal in 54 countries and in 1 country there is no law for prostitution (World Population Review, 2025). In India, prostitution is not a criminal offense but soliciting prostitution and prostitution in a public place is illegal. If prostitution is legal then sex workers could be covered under social security schemes. There are more than 8.25 lakh identified sex workers in India [one can assume 10 percent to be male and remaining females]. Not many of them want to be in this trade by choice. Many interventions have been experimented with these women. Microfinance could have become a ray of hope to many organisations and individuals. Several MFIs and other not-for-profit organisations tried to generate alternative means of livelihood for females who were into commercial sex work.

While discussing sex work is also a taboo for most in India, far inadequate research has been done in this respect. Below mentioned are some case studies that report the kind of work that is being done by not-for-profits in red-light areas as they are popularly known.

Surat is one of the only cities in the state of Gujarat to have an earmarked area Variyavi Bazaar for the commercial sex workers, what is known as the '*Red Light Area*'. There are more than 600 female sex workers in Surat city. Not many of them want to be in this trade by choice. Hence, many interventions were experimented with these women but not many showed remarkable results. NGOs gave small loans to the women or their husbands to start off alternative livelihood.

Sonagachi in Kolkota is home to Asia's largest red-light districts. Many NGOs are helping forming a collective of sex workers, Durbar, an NGO empowered them to say no to sex without condoms. The experiment was so successful that in time, 65,000 sex workers across the country would join this collective. Each day 800 young women join the trade here. USHA's a multipurpose co-operative lend to these sex workers and larger loans were made available to finance micro-enterprises (e.g., sewing, craft manufacture, small retail, farmland and livestock, investment in rickshaw or taxicab). This initiative did find moderate success.

Swathi Jyothi in Bangaluru helps build the financial literacy of women and offers them a range of financial services. Major reasons of microfinance are secure housing and education of children. Swathi Jyothi has been able to reach out to 4200 women in sex work to cater to their basic needs and start their own business and come out of sex work. It has a livelihood resource center for the members.

Sangini Women's Cooperative Bank (SWCB) in Mumbai is an initiative where more than 1700 sex workers have formed co-operative banks from savings collected from among themselves. Most importantly provided a safe locker to their savings. They have disbursed loan to members; which hitherto was impossible. It has given these women the confidence to 'SAY NO' to clients involving health hazards. Mumbai has one of the most organised sex industries in the country. However, it is always under a scanner of public, government institutions and private institutions for various reasons including may be the stigma of sharing a neighbourhood with sex workers to being blamed to be the HIV spreading agents or just the commercial value of the large expanse of land that the sex town is occupying. Today, Kamathipura is risking the evacuation of many sex workers who had made this place their address for decades together. But such is the apathy of welfare initiatives for these vulnerable groups making them even more susceptible to exploitation and misery.

The point in case here is that places like Kolkotta and Mumbai have very organised places of work for their sex workers which makes it easier to function. In contrast, the sex workers in

Ahmedabad do not have such rightful places of work which makes it difficult for them to function and more so, the phenomenon of collectivisation which could help this part of the labour force to organise and demand for welfare schemes and benefits.

It is here that the role of institutions come in particularly for cities like Ahmedabad where apparently there are so many female sex workers operating in isolation and without any much welfare initiatives and always living in a threatened environment creating pressures of different sorts.

Conclusion

Sex work has been there ever since civilisations but the nature of it changes from place to place. This has to be kept in mind while analysing the background, current conditions and future policy suggestions with respect to Female Sex Workers. Sex work in Ahmedabad may not be very organised like in many other cities of India or abroad, but none can refute the fact that it has flourished over a period of time and is evolving.

CHAPTER 5

Role of Institutions for the FSWs

Introduction

Capabilities Approach advocated by Martha Nussbaum and Amartya Sen propounds that it is important to give free Choice to individuals for achieving the various Functioning that one wants to attain from an ideal human development perspective. The Capability approach (CA) as advocated by Sen (1984) and Nussbaum (2000) connect strongly with the Human Rights approach both political and civil liberties as also the social and economic rights. The central idea of capability approach is to understand what people are effectively able to do and to be, based on their capabilities. Such understanding while designing the development policies will make a significant theoretical difference and leads to quite different policies compared to neo-liberalism and utilitarian policy prescription. Various vulnerabilities render the marginalised not being able to attain the Functionings that they desire which is basically addressed to as lack of capabilities. A lack in capabilities for instance good education, good health, adequate skill development, familial and societal support etc. hampers an individual's development and restricts the freedom in making choices that are critical. Institutions play a vital role in connecting capabilities and enhancing the freedoms available to a developing society (Drèze and Sen, 2002). In the current chapter the role of various institutions is being explored as it is taken to be the core of human development for the framework of the current study.

Institutions and FSWs in Ahmedabad

Several institutions play a significant role in enhancing capabilities in a human life like schools, colleges, health centres, religious institutions, civic administrative offices, social bodies etc. While the inquiry run in here was with specific reference to female sex workers and institutions that impact their lives and livelihoods significantly, the undercurrent remains whether these institutions support the FSWs strong enough to offer them choices to lead their lives to attain the Functionings that they deem to be appropriate. In this context, it is important to deliberate with NGOs, government bodies, police department, academic institutions, financial institutions etc.

Role of Sakhijyot as a Community Based Organisation (CBO)

Sakhijyot was established in the year 2003 (though it existed and carried on its work under the aegis of its parent organisation Jyotisangh since 1998) as a Community Based Organisation to work for the welfare of Female Sex Workers operating in Ahmedabad.

Sakhijyot is the offshoot of one of the most renowned organisations Jyotisangh which was established by the father of nation Mahatma Gandhi. It inquires into the functioning of various social, economic and heath related concerns of women. Based on its ideals of formation, Jyotisangh actively involved in formulating various programmes for women rights and their welfare from 1934 to 2010. In 1997, Jyotisangh started active campaigning and projects to curb the spread of HIV AIDS with the help of the female sex workers in Ahmedabad itself. Gradually a Targeted Intervention was designed and undertaken with the help of consultation with FSWs themselves and also DFID. Since, most cities of Gujarat do not have a specified Red-Light area the task of gathering data is very difficult for any programmes which could form as the base for many policy actions. However, as many AIDS Awareness and health welfare programmes managed by Jyotisangh for sex workers proved impactful. It helped in winning the confidence and gathering critical information. As information poured in through some studies, there was a need to address the questions of sex worker as exploitation by flesh trading brokers, policemen, social disgrace, illiteracy, lethargic towards health problems, uneven family lives, legal and social status etc. in the beginning only few female members were actively involved in the task and they formed an unorganised group which later on, in 2003, converted and registered itself as Sakhijyot, a Community Based Organisation of sex workers, by the sex workers and for the sex workers (Sakhijyot Sangathan Web, 2022).

According to one of the employees (who has worked for more than two decades in the organisation) there the women in sex work gradually become very resilient and tend to voice their opinions also very strongly as against the timid and vulnerable identities that they carried when they joined the profession due to the circumstances. Most of the women in sex work associated with the CBO had joined the profession due to dire financial crisis in their families which left not many options for them. While this profession gave them the financial support that they were seeking for their families to sustain. The institution, Sakhijyot provided the collective to represent their thoughts and concerns and took care of a lot of issues primarily and significantly pertaining to their health and security. There were only some women, according to this employee, who had been forced to join this profession by some commission agents/ brokers who would have promised them jobs and brought them to Ahmedabad city from their villages in mostly Bengal or some eastern state. Only those women may have been rescued and send back to their families if they were not willing to continue. However, some of these rescued women chose to continue in the profession as it fetches them some money to send over to their families back home where there are hardly any sustainable livelihood options. Sakhijyot has been successfully able to supply healthcare support in terms of medicines, condoms, regular health check-ups and also awareness about Sexually Transmitted Diseases and other related health disorders. On being asked to share the figures, it was informed that out of approximately 1100 women who are associated with the CBO, about 23 women have been affected by AIDS. There are counsellors who provide psychological support to distressed women in the profession. However, there are very few women who leave this work and take up any other alternative livelihood option.

The treasurer of the CBO gave significant inputs regarding detailed functioning and the resource generation and allocation at the organisation. She added that there is good funding support from various government agencies particularly the NACO.

Crisis, Non-work and Impact

During Covid-19 pandemic, the times became still tougher due to the sudden lockdown and subsequent social distancing norms. Survival became a problem for many of these women who were dependent on sex work as their livelihood. It was in such times that Community Based Organisations (CBO) like Sakhijyot play a very significant role. They negotiated ration kits and medical aid for the FSWs from the government and saw that it was distributed among these needy women. The fundamental problem that government would otherwise face in absence of a good CBO is that FSWs would not have the Identity cards that will be acknowledged for the purpose of welfare payments since most FSWs do not want to admit their profession and income in their cards like Aadhar Card.

On inquiring about the support that they would expect from agencies or would like to acknowledge, below stated was the response. It would be good to have FSWs registered in the All-India Network of Female Sex Workers since there are major benefits of doing that. The CBO could form an alliance with Global Fund and manage to get financial support, ration kits, sanitary pads and sanitizers free. This was great help according to her.

> 'ઓલ ઈન્ડિયા નેટવર્ક સેક્સ વર્કરબહેનો માટે રજીસ્ટર છે. તેમાં બહેનોને ઘણાં જ લાભો મેળવી શકે છે. ગ્લોબલ ફંડ થી અલાયન્સ દ્વારા કોવિડ-૧૯ માં ફાઈનાન્સિયલ સપોટ, રેશનકીટ, સેનેટરી પેડ, સેનીટાઈઝર જેવી મદદ મળી.'

Certain legal entities, registrations and alliances could be of great benefit to the FSWs.

The recent judgement of the Supreme Court (2022) was a milestone for the welfare of FSWs in India as sex work will now be considered as a profession and this provision would provide some dignity, protection and legality to this age-old profession and workers involved in it. It has also been expected out of the police to not make unnecessary arrests of SWs and their children should not be separated from them merely for the reason that their mother is involved in sex work. It is to be noted that only profiting from trading on others bodies is still a punishable offence and hence, pimping is an offence. However, out of their own will any woman can resort to sex work – sometimes as a compulsion to fend for her family or sometimes out of her own choice to be in this profession to earn better.

Role of Other NGOs

There are very few NGOs which are directly involved in the welfare and rehabilitation activities of Female Sex Workers in Ahmedabad city. From the investigations conducted through discussions with experts, it was found that there is only one major CBO Sakhijyot as mentioned above was involved in ameliorating the conditions of FSWs in Ahmedabad. There are a few other organisations that are involved but not dedicated totally to the cause. These organisations are associated with FSWs mainly from the point of view of their health. The Civil Hospital and many other physicians with private practice check these FSWs at their clinics. This enables the FSWs to keep a check on their health and remain active workers for long time and also not conquer sexually transmitted diseases. One of the most significant organisations that even became the contributor of establishing a Community Based Organisation for the city's FSWs is National Aids Control Organisation (NACO) and Gujarat State Aids Control Society. NACO particularly started work from the point of view of controlling AIDS in the city. FSWs were a group that formed a group for targeted intervention for protection against Sexually Transmitted Diseases (STD). FSWs were educated with regard to having safe sex, using condoms and being adamant about forcing clients to wear condoms apart from distribution of medicines and enabling treatment for HIV at the clinics tied up. NACO in various ways still financially supports the CBO for various initiatives.

Role of Microfinance and Other Financial Services Institutions

The most significant objective for the current study was how microfinance institutions could enhance the alternative livelihood opportunities for the FSWs. It has been claimed in various researches that microfinance is one of the most efficient methods of development finance with corroborated positive results for financial inclusion of vulnerable groups. The study wanted to know the role that Microfinance institutions have played in the livelihoods of FSWs in Ahmedabad. However, it is unfortunate to know that there are hardly any microfinance institutions that are financing welfare initiatives for FSWs in Ahmedabad. Most microfinance institutions may have generally addressed the issues and needs of various vulnerable groups but that does not cater to the specific needs of FSWs. There is very little or no evidence of microfinance institutions benefitting FSWs or even enhancing the alternatives of livelihood for them.

Only one initiative was close to offering some productive option to FSWs in Ahmedabad which was supported by co-operative Bank and that was way back in the year 1999 and 2000. This initiative also found little success. Whatever little was also due to the interest of Jyotisangh, Ahmedabad Municipal Corporation and Gujarat Aids Control Society, who insisted on opening a formal account representing all FSWs associated so that they have a place to park their savings, earn interest on it, take loans when need be and above all be their security for old age (Sandesh, 2000). Without this initiative, it was almost impossible to open a bank account for lack of identity proof for FSWs. Many FSWs were able to get assistance and were given training for handling the monies responsibly and productively. Earlier, their partners would otherwise squander away all the money saved since there were not many avenues to save. But it would be pitiable since generally a female sex worker could find work actively until they attain the age of 40 and after that there was no source of financial security for her. This uncertainty can be met solved if an active bank account is opened in the name of the FSWs. Moreover, it would at any point in time offer an opportunity to start an alternative livelihood opportunity with the help of loans that could be availed. However, this arrangement did not work for long.

It is inevitable to build an ecosystem in which the FSWs are also a part of inclusive growth in the society and without financial inclusion initiatives it is not possible. Financial inclusion is certainly the stepping stone to many other Sustainable Development Goals. When organised financial institutions are unable to offer these services to vulnerable sections of the society at least microfinance institutions should be able to do it otherwise the gap continues to be. However, in Ahmedabad city it has been found that there is dearth of such initiatives which could solve the financial problems of FSWs.

Table 1

Points of Deliberation	*Critical Analysis in Microfinance Institutions*	*Input for MFIs*
Identification	Any intervention which will require the FSW to divulge her professional identity on paper will find least interest from the FSW.	The idea could be the way Sakhijyot formulated a group and then do it which enables hiding individual identities.
Group formation	Who should be combined by MFIs to form JLGs/ SHGs so that the activities are sustainable for FSWs.	JLGs/SHGs should combine all members of FSW community to form a small cohesive group. However, some experts say that they have found success in grouping FSWs with people of different professions.
Financial Literacy	Awareness about financial matters.	Before beginning any microfinance activity, it is important to create awareness on savings and investments and other financial matters for FSWs and their family members too.

Points of Deliberation	*Critical Analysis in Microfinance Institutions*	*Input for MFIs*
Capacity Building	Training for skills to build capacity of FSWs.	The idea of 'choice' for profession can really be implemented if FSWs in JLGs/SHGs are trained for alternative professions – just not limited to sewing, could be small farming, driving, technical and mechanical skills etc. Any skill that could match the demand in the labour market.
Social Intermediation	Social intermediation in matters of health and well-being.	It is important to offer social intermediation not only from physical health perspective but also mental well-being of the FSW to keep microfinance activities functioning effectively. Team building activities and building stronger bonds to work for each other plus counselling services could be very helpful.

Source: Created by author based on primary study.

Role of Police in the Sector

As shared by the CBO, police raids were the most common threats to the profession of female sex workers. Therefore, it was necessary to understand from the perspective of the police what were the provisions and measures for law and order in this profession and how police could be play an affirmative role in the well-being of these women. Based on discussions with our experts, it is understood that the current position of police towards the FSWs have changed considerably than what existed in the past. Now there is much more awareness and willingness to support generally and protect, if need be, the FSWs from any untoward incidents. This assurance of police goes a long way for the FSWs, many of them who have no other alternative to go back to and fend their families (some of them are in this profession out of their own choice).

The Police along with various human rights organisations and women's right organisations work together and conduct awareness towards this profession. Trafficking is to be legally penalised but most of them are doing their work quietly on their own. Hence, it is important to differentiate between the same. Above all, it has to be now accepted by the society at large that sex work is also now among the first choice of career that many from the younger population of present generation. The police have to play a very amicable and forthcoming role in creating an environment conducive for all forms of works to prosper.

Role of Government in the Sector

The Women & Child Development Department of Government of Gujarat has played a very crucial role in advocating policies favouring the FSWs of the state. It has been instrumental in organising various workshops and awareness sessions collectively to several women occupied in sex work.

The Women & Child Development Department of Government of Gujarat organised sewing classes for the FSWs to impart them some skills that could help them keep afloat during crisis or even create a choice for an alternative livelihood for them. Approximately 1200 FSWs in and around Ahmedabad were trained under the project. Another, similar initiative some time back was a project by the United Nation called 'Me By Me', wherein FSWs were trained in photography and an exhibition was then organised. Sakhijyot, the CBO for FSWs in Ahmedabad, had initiated to formalise their earnings and savings by putting into a bank account and using it when needed (as earlier it was found difficult for the women to divulge their identity and profession) with the support of a co-operative bank that allowed the CBO to open a single account with multiple people depositing but co-ordinated by the office of the CBO. This helped many women to take loans for some other commercial activities like purchasing an autorickshaw etc. However, these arrangements did not find much success in the long run. Also, any other initiative to rehabilitate women from this profession did not find much success as once the FSWs come into this profession, after the initial struggles and stigma, they admit to appreciate the income that they are able to make from this work and refuse to leave the work as they find not only physical exploitation of women in all fronts of work but also payments to be very meagre to look after the needs of their families. In this light, it is important to improve the legislations and welfare provisions around female sex work so that they at least are saved from violence at work and receive prompt and right medical attention when needed.

On interviewing the president of the FSWs associated with the CBO Sakhijyot, below stated is what she had to state about their expectations from government.

> 'સમાજની સ્થાન મેળવવા માંગતી હોય છે સમાજની તીરછી નજરથી બચવા માંગતી હોય છે તે પણ સામાન્ય સ્ત્રી ની જેમ જ જીવન જીવવા માંગતી હોય છે. પોલીસ પણ તેમને રહેમનજરથી જોવે તેમ ઈચ્છતી હોય છે, તેમજ સરકાર પણ તેમના ડોક્યુમેન્ટ વગર પૈસે કાઢી આપે તેમ ઈચ્છે છે. તેમજ આ બહેનો વધારો ભણેલી નથી હોતી તેથી સરકાર શ્રી તરફથી અવનવી યોજનાઓમાં તાલીમ આપી તેને આજીવિકા મેળવી શકે તેવા પ્રયત્ન કરવા જોઈએ, જેથી હાઈરિસ્કમાંથી નીકળી શકે.'

Primarily the FSWs also want acceptance from the society and not to be despised by everyone. They just want to live simple and peaceful lives. They do expect that police have a sympathetic approach towards them and their work. Moreover, since it is difficult to get a lot of identity documents for women in sex work, the expectation from the government is to pay off welfare funds without such document requirements from them. Besides, most women in sex work are not very educated and so government could encourage and support by providing some vocational training with regard to alternative sustainable livelihood options so that FSWs could move out from the higher risks that they carry in their profession.

Role of Academic Institutions

During the course of the study, a panel discussion was arranged to discuss the welfare policies that could benefit FSWs in general. There was a lot of interest and discussion that was created in the minds of young students by the experts who participated in the forum. This is what academic institutions can do the least, try and remove the myths from the minds of many young students who can normalise the existence of sex workers in the society and also work for the welfare of these excluded sections of the society.

The panel discussion had a privileged start with the expert words and opinion of Prof. Gaurang Jani, retired sociologist from Gujarat University and who is an authority on the subject in Gujarat due to his long association with NACO and other development agencies- government and non-government on these issues. He shared challenges that form part of the work and personal lives of female sex workers particularly the fact that they cannot divulge their identity and therefore remain constrained from accessing many governments welfare schemes. There are some landmark judgements which did support and ameliorate the living conditions of many female sex workers especially that of Right to Food and Sex Work as profession. Prof. Jani also added that one of the research scholars consulting him on her research thesis, has documented in her finding based on the survey of more than 250 female sex workers, that more than 90 percent of women have admitted that they are into this profession since there was severe exploitation in their earlier so called 'moral and dignified' professions too. He said that various institutions including the government and academic institutions could play a vital role in supporting female sex workers.

Prof. Rajesh Mackwana from Central University of Gujarat shared his understanding and knowledge drawn from working on a project which was based on communities engaged in sex work. So, the sociology of several castes being pushed into sex work for generations is a fact that all need to realise. This also can be witnessed in some communities settled in and around Ahmedabad city too. Since, the ancestors were pushed into this profession, many are left with no choice but continue the profession because in India professions are taken forward/received from generation to generation unless there are some strong targeted interventions but this also fails most times. Therefore, supporting humans irrespective of their professions (as far as they are in the legal domain) is a very significant understanding that one has to develop.

Dr. Awa Shukla, I/c Director (Student Services), Dr. Babasaheb Ambedkar Open University spoke about the initiatives that her University had taken to educate and skill female sex workers and many other marginalised groups. Particularly, they put in efforts to bring in FSWs to study and get their degrees in an open learning environment and open schooling system which is conducive for the women who may choose to study ahead. But most FSWs want their children to study and prosper and this is a common answer which Dr. Shukla also mentioned during the discussions and something which came up during the respondent surveys too.

Dr. Ishmeet Kaur, Assistant Professor from Central University of Gujarat exerted that despite of so many discussions and some good legislations too, the gender divide is still very glaring. Women are already marginalised and female sex workers are a group that remain invisible even in these marginalised populations. It is important to come up with conducive policy for the well-being of female sex workers and particularly with respect to their education and also educating others about them.

It is important to note from expert discussions that there are various reasons and circumstances due to which women chose to be in this profession. Also, that there is this common thread of understanding and expectation that efforts need to scale up for the support towards the well-being of the FSWs from all respect.

Conclusion

This chapter outlined the role of the various institutions which could be substantial to support the Female Sex Workers in drawing their constitutional rights in a very unequal society. This means that every human being has all right to choose their work and pursue it with utmost diligence for meeting their needs, barring anything that is illegal in nature. This is where apart from awareness active participation of people's institutions is necessary to take affirmative actions and bring into the mainstream every excluded section including the FSWs.

CHAPTER 6

Conclusion and Recommendations

The female sex workers are a very marginalised and vulnerable segment in India and similarly so it is in Ahmedabad too. It is unfortunate that very few institutions are showing active interest and even lesser taking initiatives and designing projects for welfare of FSWs. It was in this light that this study becomes significant.

There is a significant population in Ahmedabad city depending on FSWs for their bodily needs and this is evident from the number of FSWs functioning in the city. However, the society is not waking up to the fact that this is one of the oldest professions existing in the world and the workers forming a part of this profession too need to be treated equally with fair access to all constitutional rights and not harassed for any choices of work that she makes or has had to make forcibly many times.

There are many recommendations that came up during the course of the current study. It may be required from different agencies and different perspectives. It is summarised in the following section.

First and foremost is the expectation of FSWs from the government, which is the most significant arm of treating all citizens fairly and equally. The government departments, particularly the Women and Child Development Department should scale up the activities that they engage from the point of view of female sex workers and should be taken up more sustainably. Sustainability is significant since many a times the budgets are not responsive enough to take care of these excluded sections and their welfare needs. So, it is very easy to start some initiative and then leave it off when there is shortage of funds for such initiatives. This has been the apathy of many projects; they are short-lived that they may not really show any significant impact especially from livelihood point of view for such vulnerable segments. Hence, when this profession is legally recognised there is more that can be done for female sex workers in terms of welfare provisions particularly as revealing their identities also become a threat for them to stay amicably in the society.

The FSWs are High-Risk communities from the point of view of their health and apparently their capability of spreading communicable diseases. NACO along with various NGOs supporting FSWs has been doing a good job with respect to providing medical aid and treatments through targeted intervention. Even in Ahmedabad, one can find strong evidences of this. In fact, whatever little movement in organising and tracing FSWs in Ahmedabad began with NACOs project on AIDS Control through Jyoti Sangh. The peer educators in the project did a wonderful job in creating awareness about health and rights among the FSWs. This kind of resource allocation in terms of people and funds are needed to directly address the challenges and vulnerabilities of FSWs. Another recommendation in the same vein is that health has to be looked at from a holistic perspective and not only for the prevention of communicative diseases. Each individual FSW is precious and a citizen of India having all rights to public resources and infrastructure, keeping this in mind, a holistic health programme catering to their immunity, well being and security in the old age and ill-health of FSWs.

The study primarily was started with the intention of whether microfinance institutions have been of help to provide small financial support needed to create and pursue choices of alternative livelihood for the FSWs. But the entire exercise was an eye opener from the perspective of inclusiveness in development finance because there is hardly and sustained microfinance programme supporting with dedicated efforts the target segment of FSWs in such a huge city of Ahmedabad. Hence, a strong recommendation is from this end that unless development finance institutions particularly MFIs are offering direct support to FSWs, none can boast of reaching the last person in the population with financial aid. Ahmedabad strongly lacks this financial support to the FSW segment.

Long discussions with Prof. Gaurang Jani brought out the need strongly for a 'Single Point' window for signature required for sanctioning payments for various government social security schemes since they lack identity cards of any forms that would divulge their profession and other details. Only then there could be access to welfare schemes designed by government for all marginalised sections including the sex workers.

One common thread of recommendation that came down from all FSWs is that they want the police especially and society generally to be more empathetic towards them so that they can continue their profession peacefully because ultimately this is their major mainstay for earning and keeping their families. This approach needs to be cultivated in public in India through various discussions and awareness programmes. The media also could play a strong role. It needs to reverse the image and perceptions created since long about the FSWs.

From the point of view of research, it is also significant that future studies on FSWs take up family as a unit of analysing and not just the individual since it is the entire family which is impacted by the choice of profession and generally supports the women involved in sex work.

On being asked to most women in sex work about what they want for future or for their children, they have a very unanimous answer to this that they want their children to be educated and take up professions that will be valued and rewarded adequately.

> 'બહેનો ઈચ્છે છે કે પોતાના બાળકો સારું ભણી-ગણીને સારી જગ્યાએ નોકરી કરે અને એમનું ભવિષ્ય ઉજ્જવળ બને.'

This is where education institutions have a vital role to play. There is a need to design more inclusive environments in terms of admissions and teaching-learning environments that do not discriminate based on the social, economic or professional backgrounds of parents or self while educating each and all.

References

A tainted tradition (2013). http://issuesindia.hpage.co.in/rehab-of-sws_59748541.html The Hindu. March 23, 2013.

Agwu, P., Okoye, U., Ekoh, P., Chukwu, N., Onalu, C., Igwe, I., Onuh, P., Amadi, G. and Nche, G. (2020). 'A systematic review of drivers and interventions against sex work migration in Edo State, Nigeria', *International Journal of Sociology and Social Policy,* Vol. 40 No. 7/8, pp. 733–764. https://doi.org/10.1108/IJSSP-03-2020-0097

Ahmedabad City Population (2011). https://www.census2011.co.in/census/city/314-ahmedabad.html

Aideyan, Osaore (2013). Bergamo Microfinance and Poverty Reduction in Rural Nigeria. Savings and Development, Vol. 33, No. 3 (2009), pp. 293–317. *Research Center on International Cooperation of the University of Bergamo.* http://www.jstor.org/stable/41406498.

Badatya, K.C. Wadavi, B.B. and Ananti, S., NABARD (2006). Microfinance to Microenterprises: An Impact evaluation Study of Self-Help Groups. *Evaluation Report of NABARD,* 2006.

Boroumandfar, Z., Esmaeili, R. and Mohaghegh, N. (2022). The Story of Female Sex Workers in The Shadow of Sex Work Coercion: A Qualitative Study. Iranian *Journal of Nursing and Midwifery Research,* Vol.27 Issue 3.

CGAP (2024). Financial Inclusion. Available at https://www.cgap.org/financial-inclusion

ChartsBin Statistics Collector team (2010). The legal Status of Prostitution by Country. ChartsBin.com. http://chartsbin.com/view/snb http://timesofindia.indiatimes.com/city/surat/Welfare-in-mind-sex-workers-form-NGOs/articleshow/4071880.cms

Chauhan, Srishti (2022). Financial Inclusion in India: Inching Close to the Last Mile. EACPM Working Paper Series. Available at https://eacpm.gov.in/wp-content/uploads/2023/07/3-Financial-Inclusion-Srishti-Chauhan.pdf

Coetzee, J. (2023). Understanding drivers of female sex workers' experiences of external/enacted and internalised stigma: findings from a cross-sectional community-centric national study in South Africa. Culture, Health & Sexuality, 25(11), 1433–1448.

Department for International Development Report (2004). Prevalence and trend of Sexually Transmitted Infections and HIV among

Female Sex Workers of Ahmedabad, Gujarat, India, During 2000–2003, p. 17.

DFID Report (1999). Sex Industry and Commercial Sex Workers of Ahmedabad (presented to Ahmedabad AIDS Control Society), p. 10.

Drèze, Jean and Sen, Amartya (2002). India: Development and Participation. Oxford: Oxford University Press.

Economic empowerment for women in sex work.
http://indiamicrofinance.com/y/swathi-jyothi

Fatima, Soofia (2024). Microfinance in India-A Catalyst of Financial Inclusion and Economic Growth: With Special Reference to Bihar. *International Journal for Multidisciplinary Research.* https://www.researchgate.net/publication/381917128_Microfinance_in_India-A_Catalyst_of_Financial_Inclusion_and_Economic_Growth_With_Special_Reference_to_Bihar.

Fisher & Sriram (2008). Beyond microcredit Putting Development Back into Microfinance, Vistaar Publications, New Delhi, Oxfam Oxford, UK, New Economics Foundation, London, p. 49.

Green Light for Red Light Areas' Accessed 23rd May, 2023. http://indialegalonline.com/green-light-red-light-areas/

Jewkes, R., Milovanovic, M., Otwombe, K., Hlongwane, K., Hill, N. and Mbowane, V., ...

Khursheed, Ambreen (2022). Exploring the role of microfinance in women's empowerment and entrepreneurial development: A qualitative study. *Future Business Journal,* Vol.8, Issue 57.

KPMG Report (2019). Microfinance Contributions to Financial Inclusion, Opportunities and Challenges Ahead.
https://assets.kpmg.com/content/dam/kpmg/in/pdf/2019/12/MFI-Microfinance-contributions-to-financial-inclusion.pdfa

Lwesya, F. and Mwakalobo, A.B.S. Frontiers in microfinance research for small and medium enterprises (SMEs) and microfinance institutions (MFIs): A Bibliometric Analysis. *Future Business Journal.* Vol. 9, Issue 17.

Mayengbam, Chingkheinganbi (2022). SC wants dignity for Sex Workers: Where is prostitution most prevalent in India? India Today, May 27, 2022.
https://www.indiatoday.in/diu/story/sex-workers-india-most-prevalent-in-southern-states-1955146-2022-05-27

Mbonye M, Nalukenge W, Nakamanya S, Nalusiba B, King R, Vandepitte J, Seeley J. Gender inequity in the lives of women involved in sex work in Kampala, Uganda. *J Int AIDS Soc.* 2012 Jun 14; 15 Suppl 1(Suppl 1):1-9. doi: 10.7448/IAS.15.3.17365.

Meki, Muhammad and Quinn, Simon (2024). Microfinance; An Overview. Oxford Review of Economic Policy, Volume 40, Issue 1, Spring 2024, Pages 1–7. https://doi.org/10.1093/oxrep/grae004

Miles, G.M., Blase, O., Clark, K., Ding, R.J. and Geyer, T. (2020), "Don't look down on us!': Assessing the vulnerabilities of female massage parlor workers in Phnom Penh, Cambodia', *International Journal of Sociology and Social Policy*, Vol. 40 No. 1/2, pp. 20–43. https://doi.org/10.1108/IJSSP-01-2019-0017.

Morduch, J. (1999). The Micro Finance Promise, Journal of Economic Literature, 37 (4): 1569–1614.

National Strategy for Financial Inclusion (2018). Available at Securities Exchange Board of India: https://www.sebi.gov.in/National_Strategy_for_Financial_Inclusion.html

Nayak, Abhay (2011). Economic empowerment for women in sex work through Microfinance accessed from http://Indiamicrofinance.com/economic-empowerment-women-sex-work-microfinance.html

Nussbaum, M.C. (2000). Woman and Human Development: The capabilities approach. Cambridge University Press, Cambridge.

Ozili, P.K. and Syed, A.A. (2024). Financial inclusion and fintech research in India: A Review. Munich Personal RePEc Archive. https://mpra.ub.uni-muenchen.de/121526/1/MPRA_paper_121526.pdf

Pachauri, S., Pachauri, A. and Mittal, K. (2022). Female Sex Work Dynamics: Empowerment, Mobilization, Mobility. In: Sexual and Reproductive Health and Rights in India. Springer Briefs in Public Health. Springer, Singapore. https://doi.org/10.1007/978-981-16-4578-5_4

Pattnaik, D., Ray, Sougata and Hassan, K.M (2024). Microfinance: A bibliometric exploration of the knowledge landscape. Heliyon. Vol. 10, Issue 10.

Potter, K., Martin, J. and Romans, S. (1999). Early developmental experiences of female sex workers: a comparative study. *The Australian and New Zealand Journal of Psychiatry*, Vol. 33, Issue 6.

Prostitution in India-Make it Legal'. http://www.economist.com/news/asia/21629472-proper-debate-needed-legalising-sex-work-make-it-legal

Raccanello, K, Anand, J. and Santos, A.V. (2011). Collateral Ownership and Women's Participation in Informal Finance Schemes. *International Journal of Microfinance;* Vol. 1, No. 1. pp. 14–24.

Rawls, John (2001). Justice as Fairness: A Restatement, Cambridge, Massachusetts: Belknap Press.

RBI (2021). Financial Inclusion – Past, Present and Future. htps://www.bis.org/review/r210715c.pdf

RBI Bulletin (2021). Financial Inclusion Index for India. Speech of Shakti Kanta Das: https://rbi.org.in/scripts/BS_ViewBulletin.aspx?Id=20502

Red lights may go out of Surat's Chakla Bazaar' http://timesofindia.indiatimes.com/city/ahmedabad/Red-lights-may-go-out-of-Surats-Chakla-Bazaar/articleshow/180655.cms

Reserve Bank of India Report (2018). Report on Trend and Progress of Banking in India. June, 2018, pp. 82.

Sakhijyot Sangathan History.
http://sakhijyot.org/historical-tour/

Sandesh (2000). New banking service started for Female Sex Workers in the city. Sandesh Gujarati Daily News Paper, 23rd June, 2000. Friday, Ahmedabad.

Scott, W. Richard (2004). 'Institutional theory.' In Encyclopedia of Social Theory, George Ritzer, ed. Thousand Oaks, CA: Sage, pp. 408–414.

Sen, Amartya (1984). Rights and Capabilities. In Resources, Values and Development. Cambridge, Mass: Harvard University Press.

Sex Workers of Kamathipura: Nowhere to Go, Nowhere to Live. https://www.outlookindia.com/magazine/national/sex-workers-of-gangubai-kamathipura-nowhere-to-go-nowhere-to-live-magazine-184855

Swallow, Y.C., Patnam, M. and Haksar, V. (2021). A digital infrastructure known as the India Stack is revolutionizing access to finance. https://www.imf.org/external/pubs/ft/fandd/2021/07/india-stack-financial-access-and-digital-inclusion.htm

Swendeman *et al.* (2009). Empowering sex workers in India to reduce vulnerability to HIV and sexually transmitted diseases.
http://www.ncbi.nlm.nih.gov/pmc/articles/PMC2824563/

UNDP (2012). Global Commission on HIV and the Law, Risks, Rights & Health, p. 41.

Woman's Rights—The principle of gender equality is enshrined in the Indian Constitution. Retrieved from https://www.legalserviceindia.com/helpline/woman_rights.htm

World Bank Group (2024). Overview: Financial Inclusion is a key enabler to reducing poverty and boosting prosperity. Available at https://www.worldbank.org/en/topic/financialinclusion/overview#:~:text=Financial%20inclusion%20means%20that%20individuals,Sustainable%20Development%20Goals%20(SDGs)

World Population Review (2025). Countries where Prostitution is Legal 2025: https://worldpopulationreview.com/country-rankings/countries-where-prostitution-is-legal

Yunus, Muhammad (1999). Banker to the Poor: Micro-lending and the battle against world poverty. Public Affairs, New York.

List of Acronyms

AIDS	:	Acquired Immunodeficiency Syndrome
AMC	:	Ahmedabad Municipal Corporations
BC	:	Business Correspondent Model
CBO	:	Community Based Organisation
CEDAW	:	Convention on the Elimination of All Forms of Discrimination Against Women
DFID	:	Department for International Development
FII	:	Financial Inclusion Index
FSW	:	Female Sex Workers
HIV	:	Human Immunodeficiency Virus
MFI	:	Microfinance Institution
NABARD	:	National Bank for Agriculture and Rural Development
NACO	:	National AIDS Control Organisation
NGO	:	Non-Government Organisation
RBI	:	Reserve Bank of India
STD	:	Sexually Transmitted Diseases
SW	:	Sex Worker
TI	:	Targeted Intervention
WHO	:	World Health Organisation